THE ICE AGE

The Revolutionary Period For Basketball In San Antonio

TOM – TOM

For ordering, booking, permission, or questions, contact the author.

ISBN-13: **978-1530097104**

ISBN-10: **153009710X**

Printed in the United States of America by Create Space

Dedication

First and foremost, I would like to thank God for giving me the vision and lining up the proper channels to make this book happen for me.

This book is a general dedication to all of Spurs Nation – Spurs fans from all over the world, especially the long-suffering fans who were around from the very beginning - through the down years until the team finally had their breakthrough.

Table Of Contents

Introduction

Unfortunately, I didn't get the chance to watch George Gervin play basketball because I was too young to understand and enjoy basketball when he played. I started watching sports roughly around the mid 80's as a little kid, right when The Iceman was leaving the NBA - his last season (with the Bulls) came when I was in kindergarten. By the time I started getting old enough to understand what I was watching, David Robinson was the man in San Antonio.

I became a Spurs historian when I was 16 years old, and it was at that time that I realized that I missed out on watching the first great Spur, and one of the great scorers of all-time. The more highlights I watched, the more I came to see that The Iceman was poetry in motion. He was a lights-out scorer that had an uncanny ability to make the game look easy. Ice was as graceful and acrobatic a player as you could find, with an abundance of ways to put the ball in the basket. Whether it was his smooth jump shot or trademark finger-roll, it always looked effortless for him.

Instead of the finger-roll and the scoring titles, the first things that come to my mind about George Gervin are his NBA career average of 26.2 points per game and him doing it on 51% shooting. One other thing the Spurs/Ice fans should know, is that in addition to being on of the bridges between the ABA and the modern NBA, he had a hand in the globalization of the league. Ice and Bob McAdoo were the first big-name players to go overseas and play basketball. When Ice played, the media wasn't nearly as involved as it is today, and the technology wasn't there. If the world had a chance to see The Iceman and the other superstars of his era, they would probably be looked at differently.

Since I was born in 1979, I didn't know much about the George Gervin-era Spurs before doing research for this book, other than those were some high-scoring teams. After watching a lot of old games and hours of watching highlights and reading books, I have a much better understanding of The Iceman's legacy and how he transcended the game, as well as a keen awareness that several of his accomplishments don't fit the narrative of him being strictly a scorer - as he's made out to be. Learning all of these things about George Gervin has also led to me developing a deeper appreciation for him and his contributions to the Spurs and the game of basketball in general. I also credit Ice for all of the championships that the Spurs have won, because without him being there to pioneer the franchise, none of it would be possible.

1

The Early Years

George Gervin, like the 2 Spurs franchise players that came after him, took a unique path to the NBA. One of 6 children, he grew up in an impoverished, single-parent home in Detroit after his father left home when he was a toddler. Before basketball was on his radar he had ambitions of being a police officer. Ice was introduced to basketball when he was a teenager as an effective way to channel his energies. Ice has said that he ran the streets like any other kid, but the only difference was that he was addicted to basketball.

As a 5'8" sophomore, Ice tried out for the basketball team at Martin Luther King High School. He could move well, but his shot needed some work. Initially the team's head coach told his assistant coach, Willie Meriweather who was the junior varsity team's coach, to cut Ice. Since Coach Meriweather took a liking to Ice, he talked the varsity coach into letting him carry an extra player on the JV squad. As the 2 of them grew close, Ice also became friends with the school's janitor, who would let him use the gym every night as long as he would sweep up before he left.

While Ice improved his game by leaps and bounds, he also hit a growth spurt, making him 6'4" by his junior year. He struggled to stay eligible that season and missed half the games that season. He was able to get it all together for his senior year, averaging 31 points and 20 rebounds, leading his team to the state quarterfinals. After graduating from high school, Ice got a scholarship from Long Beach State to play for Jerry Tarkanian. The culture shock from being in Southern California was too much for him, so he went back home before the fall semester was over.

Ice transferred to Eastern Michigan University, where as a sophomore he averaged 29.5 points per game from the small forward spot. His reason for the move was that EMU had a lot of players he either played with or against in high school and he thought he would mesh well with them. Ice would play 39 games for EMU, averaging 26.8 points and 14.4 games, and establishing a legacy as arguably their greatest player ever. Just as Ice's career was getting back on track, he punched Roanoke College player Jay Piccola during an NCAA Division II tournament game. He was suspended for the following season, and eventually left the team. Also as a consequence for his actions, invitations to try out for the Olympics and Pan-American teams were withdrawn. EMU coach Jim Dutcher also resigned.

After Ice was suspended from basketball, he dropped out of school and went to play for the Pontiac Chaparrals in the Eastern Basketball Association, where he was spotted by former NBA player and coach Johnny Kerr, who was a scout for the Virginia Squires. After seeing Ice score 50 points in one of those games, Kerr went back and told the Squires about the skinny kid (6'7", 180 lbs.) with the soft shooting touch. The Squires signed him for $40,000 a year on January 26, 1973, which was about halfway through the season.

The 1972-73 Squires already had a star in Julius Erving, a 2nd year small forward out of the University of Massachusetts. Ice averaged 14.1 points per game in 23 minutes for the rest of that season while Dr. J (31.9 PPG) won the ABA scoring title. Squires guard Fatty Taylor was the one that came up with the "Iceman" nickname, which evolved from Iceberg Slim. The nickname referred to Ice's composure on the basketball court. Ice was off to a good start to the 1973-74 season with the Squires, averaging 25.4 points and 8.5 rebounds per game. He would play 49 games for the Squires that season before his controversial trade to the Spurs, who took the Squires to court after they tried to back out of the deal.

2
The Franchise-Saving Lawsuit

It's been said that Earl Foreman, the Virginia Squires owner, had the most creative mind in the ABA. He never had any money, but always had plenty of ideas. His financial situation was so dire at one point that he was about to cancel a Squires game against the Pacers because he owed $2,000 on the team's uniforms and they were about to be repossessed. Foreman called Pacers owner Dick Tinkham to break the news to him, but they met up and Tinkham made a last-minute save after the sheriff showed up to get the uniforms. The game was too important to him because the Pacers had a full house that night and cancelling the game wasn't an option. Tinkham was even willing to give the Squires the Pacers' road uniforms for the game if need be. Eventually, Foreman paid the bill for the uniforms, but more than likely he had to sell a player to do it.

Earl Foreman assumed a $500,000 debt when he bought his franchise in 1970. He tried to get rid of that debt over the next 4 years by selling Rick Barry, Swen Nater, Julius Erving, and eventually George Gervin. In January of 1974, word got around the ABA that the Squires were having severe financial problems. Foreman was looking to sell the team, but at the same time wanted what he could get for the players first. The Squires' financial troubles played right into the Spurs' hands. While they were struggling to stay afloat, Red McCombs and Angelo Drossos were on a mission to make moves designed to get fans interested in going to Spurs games. They believed the team needed a box-office attraction, which led to their pursuit of The Iceman.

A month after the Swen Nater deal, Drossos reached out to Earl Foreman after he heard Foreman was having money problems again. At first, Foreman was open to another deal as long as it wasn't for George Carter, who was the Squires' best player at that time. After Drossos made it clear that he wanted George Gervin, Foreman was reluctant because the Squires were hosting the upcoming ABA All-Star Game in Norfolk, VA and he didn't want the fans to boycott the game once they found out Ice was traded.

Drossos then suggested they do a delayed-delivery deal, which Foreman agreed to. The Spurs would pay $225,000 to the Squires immediately, but the trade wouldn't be effective until after the All-Star Game. The whole arrangement was kept a secret until the game. This is how the transaction was described in Jan Hubbard's **The History Of The San Antonio Spurs**:

"The owner [Foreman] said, 'I've got to have cash,'" McCombs said in a recent interview. "So we call Frost Bank [in San Antonio] and tell them 'you gotta get a guy and take this cash to National Airport in Washington, D.C., and go to a [designated] phone booth.' And we'd been given the instructions as to how we had to deliver the money. [The courier was told] 'wait for that phone to ring and when it does, the guy's going to tell you where to go next.' So it was really like a CIA kind of a program."

Drossos told Terry Pluto in **Loose Balls** that he knew that Earl Foreman would trade Ice for the same reason he traded all those other star players - he needed the money. By the time the All-Star Game was to be played, rumors had started spreading about the trade and Foreman was starting to feel some heat about it. The city of Norfolk was also going crazy over it.

During the game, Foreman started to feel some remorse about the deal and wanted to back out of it, but the problem was that it was done 2 months prior. He even told Ice after the game that he would be a Virginia Squire no matter what. Also after the game, Drossos went to Foreman to suggest a press conference to announce the deal, but Foreman told him that he couldn't go through with it, and that he told ABA commissioner Mike Storen about it since the deal was illegal.

Already not happy about the dismantling of the Squires, Storen stepped in and tried to block the deal, saying it was "detrimental to the league, and to the financial viability of the Virginia Squires franchise." He claimed that by trading the team's last legitimate star, the team was having a fire sale, which is when a franchise trades its best and most expensive players to cut costs. Earl Foreman couldn't afford to keep the Squires, but Storen wanted to find a buyer. He felt that if Foreman kept trading players for money, there would be no assets left to attract a buyer.

Storen publicly announced that he was freezing the Virginia Squires roster and that he would not approve of the deal. He also tried to offer Angelo Drossos a compromise. Storen told Drossos that he could have his choice of any player on the Squires roster except George Gervin, as well as his money back with 10% interest as a penalty on Earl Foreman, attorney fees, and he could even have George Carter if he wanted him. Neither side would budge. Drossos even told Storen that he didn't have the power to nix the trade, then threatened him with the necessary legal action to force the Squires to finish the transaction.

Here are a couple of quotes from Commissioner Storen from the press conference to show his mindset:

"San Antonio will have to learn to obey the rules of the league just like all the rest of the other teams in the league."

"I intend to make sure that George Gervin remains a Squire until when and if a new organization takes over ownership of the organization."

Right after the All-Star Game, the Squires were in Salt Lake City to play the Utah Stars. Ice was caught in the crossfire of the battle between the Spurs, the Squires, and the ABA. He was told by the league to play for the Squires. Drossos called Ice and told him he would be arrested by federal marshals on the spot if he stepped on the court that night because the Spurs had his contract. Ice called his agent, Irwin Weiner and told him what happened. Then Weiner called Drossos to find out if he really had Ice's contract. Then Drossos told Weiner that he would protect Ice from legal action if the Squires or the ABA tried to sue Ice for breach of contract. Then Ice and his agent went to San Antonio, where they eventually negotiated a new contract.

On February 1, 1974, the Spurs filed a lawsuit against Earl Foreman and the Virginia Squires in federal court in San Antonio, where the case was assigned to U.S. District Judge Adrian Spears. The Spurs were suing for breach of contract and seeking a temporary restraining order to keep the Squires from interfering with Ice playing for the Spurs. Commissioner Storen formally announced that same day in a conference call that the deal wasn't approved, following with a telegram saying, "The Virginia Squires retain title to the player." Storen also intervened in the suit.

The Spurs were adamant about bringing The Iceman to San Antonio. They arranged to have him secretly fly to San Antonio, where they hid him in a hotel under a false name. They also wanted to keep Ice away from snooping reporters who tried to prove the rumors about him already being in San Antonio. There was some newspaper speculation that he might have taken a flight to New York with the intention of going over to the NBA, which was some well-placed misinformation.

After Ice missed the game in Utah, Commissioner Storen sent Angelo Drossos a telegram saying, "Every game that Gervin is in your town, you will foreit it, If the player doesn't report back to Virginia tomorrow, you will be suspended from the league." Drossos sent back a telegram saying, "(Bleep) you, a stronger letter will follow."

Outraged at how the situation was playing out, Judge Spears granted a 10-day to the Spurs on February 6. He wrote in the injunction, **"I hate to see a man handled like can goods. Unfortunately, the one most directly concerned,**

Mr. Gervin, has not even been made a party to this suit, and it must be disconcerting to him, to say the least, for his name to be bandied about while this controversy over where he is to play, and who for, is being pursued in the courts." The court order said Ice couldn't play for any other ABA team for the next 10 days, which covered 5 games. Commissioner Storen told Red McCombs after the hearing, "No court will uphold this. You just lost your money."

While all of that was going on, Earl Foreman had found a buyer for the Squires, but the deal was contingent on Ice staying with the Squires. The Squires' buyers had intentions to present the tentative contract to the ABA's board of trustees for approval. On February 6, the local papers reported that Ice was in San Antonio to negotiate a Spurs contract pending the outcome of the suit.

Judge Spears scheduled hearings on the suit from February 11-15, and heard from everybody from Angelo Drossos to Mike Storen, to Spurs coach Tom Nissalke. For whatever reason, Foreman didn't attend the hearing. The papers reported that even his lawyers didn't have an idea of his whereabouts. His money problems were getting worse. In fact, on February 21, his lawyers filed a suit against him in state court for not paying their $5,000 retainer. Then the Phoenix Suns sued him for the $10,000 he owed them for an exhibition game.

On February 15, Judge Spears issued a preliminary injunction that Ice could stay with the Spurs temporarily, with an announcement that he would decide on the permanent injunction request within 10 days. Ice was allowed to play 2 more games for the Spurs. At some point during this process, he became convinced that he wanted to be in San Antonio.

Ice said in a local paper that Earl Foreman had treated him **"like a horse for sale"**. He also had this to say about his new team, **"The Spurs have good, solid ownership and they run a ball club like it should be run."** Ironically, he gave them a scare when he missed practice March 5 to go back to Virginia.............so he could pick up his car and break the lease on his apartment.

On March 6, Judge Spears made the injunction permanent. According to Red McCombs, the hearing wasn't one-sided. It even went into a 2nd day, listening to arguments. McCombs has also said that he was pessimistic and thought the Spurs would lose the case. Judge Spears began by pointing out that George Gervin was with the Spurs because the Squires had not paid back the $225,000 given to them in the deal. Here is the rest of the story on the ruling according to Steve Pierce in the *San Antonio Lawyer Magazine*:

The ABA by-laws provided that the Commissioner "shall hear and finally decide any dispute" to which a player is a party, and that "all disputes between Member Clubs . . . shall be settled by the Commissioner." Judge Spears found that there was no dispute between the Spurs and the Squires "until the Commissioner injected himself into the matter by persuading Foreman to refuse to deliver the player to the Spurs." (The Squires had alleged that the Spurs had breached the contract, but Foreman never showed up to testify about it.) The bylaws further empowered the Commissioner to cancel or terminate any contract, after notice and a hearing. Judge Spears found that only informal discussions were held, for the most part, on the run, between hotels and hallways, and that could not be considered a full and fair hearing. Finally, Judge Spears noted that the bylaws allowed that the Commissioner could reassign a player to another member club, provided that such a decision was approved and ratified by a vote of at least three-fourths of the member clubs, leaving open the possibility that the Commissioner could still try to undo the Gervin deal. (This perhaps had already been attempted in the March 4 marathon meeting, but in any event, it was not attempted again.) Attorney Larry Macon recalled, "There were only ten teams in the league, and the subject team got to vote, too. Drossos had at least two other teams that would always vote with him, so it would have been impossible for Storen to get the three-fourths vote he needed." No appeal was taken from the order. McCombs recalled that, after the ruling, Storen, figuring he'd been home-towned, told him, "I'll never be in a courthouse against you in San Antonio again."

Judge Spears also told ABA officials that even though the league is a legitimate business with bylaws that had been agreed to by all parties,**"You're not going to tell a man where he can work and where he can't."** In other words, the ruling was that Commissioner Storen didn't have the authority to block a legal deal, and the Virginia Squires had to live up to the agreement. According to Red McCombs, Judge Spears had one last message for the commissioner and ABA legal team: "Furthermore gentlemen, we have a new jail here and we've got plenty of room in it. And before you even consider appealing, you might want to remember we've got a place to put you." Nobody appealed the ruling, and George Gervin was a Spur.

According to Angelo Drossos, after Storen lost in court, he tried to take Drossos to court at the league level. Drossos had a strong backer in Charlie Finley, the owner of the Memphis franchise. He felt like Drossos deserved credit for being willing to spend money on improving his team instead of being taken to court. Drossos would hear from Storen one last time a few years later with a letter saying, "You may have Gervin now, but you'll never keep him as long as there's justice in the courts of Texas. Affectionately, Mike Storen." The Virginia Squires never recovered. They folded 2 years later, shortly before the merger with the NBA.

Timeline Of An Unusual Deal

January 29-30, 1974: At the ABA All-Star Game in Norfolk, VA, rumors are spreading around that Virginia Squires owner Earl Foreman has sold George Gervin, the league's 4th leading scorer, to the San Antonio Spurs. Nobody involved with either team would confirm the rumors on either day.

January 30: The Associated Press reports that Gervin has been sold to the Spurs. ABA Commissioner Mike Storen denies any knowledge of the sale, but reports say he would veto any sale in the best interests of the team and the league.

January 31: Gervin remains with the Squires, but reports indicate that Foreman has paid a $250,000 debt he was unable to pay a month earlier. Spurs trustee

Angelo Drossos and general manager Jack Ankerson meet with Storen and Foreman about a purchase of Squires forward George Carter, but nothing is decided.

February 1: The Spurs file suit in U.S. Western District Court in San Antonio against Foreman and the Squires, alleging the Squires reneged on the deal to sell Gervin to the Spurs.

February 3: Gervin leaves the Squires, who are in Salt Lake City for a game with the Utah Stars.

February 6: U.S. District Judge Adrian Spears issues a restraining order stating that Gervin cannot play for any other ABA team for the next 10 days. It also prevents the league from doing anything about the situation for the same period of time. The Spurs hold a news conference to announce that Gervin will play for the team for at least the next five games, and he will wear #44.

February 7: Gervin starts and scores 12 points as the Spurs fall to the Stars, 86-83.

February 8: Foreman sells the Squires to a group of Norfolk businessmen, who say their first move will be to regain Gervin.

February 15: After a week of hearings, Spears says he will have a decision on the case within 10 days, and "possibly sooner." He says his previous order will be extended for 10 more days, giving Gervin two more games with the Spurs. In testimony, Storen says he had offered Drossos a compromise - Virginia would keep Gervin and give the Spurs back the $225,000 plus interest and attorney's fees, and the Spurs also would get Carter. Drossos agreed, but the Squires' new owners vetoed it.

February 19: Spears grants a preliminary injunction in favor of the Spurs, saying Storen did not have the authority to block the deal. League sources say Storen probably will not pursue the matter further.

March 6: Spears grants the Spurs a permanent injunction, allowing Gervin to remain with the team.

The Iceman said that being held in basketball limbo for a month was a weird experience for him. He said he felt like a fugitive from basketball. Nobody was happier than he was when the ruling was finally issued. Here's a quote from Ice about his readiness to play after the ruling:

"I'm happy to be here and ready to play. I don't think it will be that big of an adjustment. I don't know the exact plays and all that. But I know how to play basketball."

Ice didn't even want to go to San Antonio at first. After Dr. J was traded, he became the face of the Squires. The fans, and even the ABA liked him in that capacity as well. But Ice said that he knew he found a home with the Spurs once he saw how passionate the fans were about the team. That court ruling was the key moment in Spurs history. If Ice would have never played for the Spurs, more than likely they would have either moved to another city or folded.

Side Note: *George Gervin was drafted in the 3rd round (40th overall) by the Phoenix Suns in the 1974 NBA Draft, but never played a game for them, choosing to stay with the Spurs.*

3
Putting A City On The Map

After becoming a pro basketball player at age 19, George Gervin went on to put together this resume:

-ABA All-Rookie first Team (1973)
-3x ABA All-Star (1974-1976)
-2x All-ABA Second Team (1975-1976)
-ABA All-Time Team

-9x NBA All-Star (1977-1985)
-NBA All-Star Game MVP (1980)
-5x All-NBA First Team (1978-1982)
-2x All-NBA Second Team (1977, 1983)
-4x NBA Scoring Champion (1978-1980, 1982)
-Jersey #44 Retired (Spurs)
-NBA's 50th Anniversary All-Time Team
-Basketball Hall Of Fame (1996)

George Gervin was the original sports icon in Central and South Texas. Before him there was nothing, and without him, that's likely what we would have in San Antonio today. The Iceman took San Antonio from a city that had no natural affinity for basketball or any real basketball tradition to a city of crazed, rabid fans for their only professional sports team. Because of him, Spurs games are now the entertainment mecca of San Antonio, as well as a national flagship to the world. **NOBODY** expected the Spurs to become as wildly successful as they have been. The Spurs, or the ABA for that matter, weren't even supposed to last a year. Here's a question to ponder: **Would the Spurs have even been one of the teams to make the jump to the NBA without The Iceman?** I don't know if they would even be in position to make the move.

Ice's groundbreaking game and unbelievable shot-making ability showed the people of San Antonio that basketball was a game played by some of the greatest athletes in the world, not just as a sport to fool around with when football was out of season. He introduced to the city a fast-paced game of grace, precision, and athleticism that could get your blood racing and emotions involved.

Ice gave the fans some great entertainment value for the price of their tickets. In every single game he played, there was at least 1 impossibly creative play he made that could be considered the play that "paid for your ticket." Not many players, past or present, can be put in that category. Ice was also the coolest cat to ever step foot on a basketball court, which to this day is still an appeal that was key to the Spurs' survival.

There's more to doing for your franchise than just winning championships. Don't get me wrong, that's the ultimate goal when you talk about on-court performance, but value to a franchise is about what you bring to the table on **AND** off the court. Ice was the face of the Spurs, and in a lot of respects the city. He was *the* reason people watched the Spurs for years, the reason why the Spurs got any national coverage, and of course.......the reason the team stayed in San Antonio. Ice was also the X-factor in creating a strong bond between the Spurs and the city, which has become a way of life in San Antonio. Ice's impact goes way beyond what he did on the court. He did so much for the Spurs off the court as well.

Here are some quotes that prove that George Gervin is basketball royalty:

"George Gervin was to San Antonio what Babe Ruth was to New York. Babe Ruth was baseball in New York City. He was the Yankees. Gervin was the San Antonio Spurs. He was the symbol of basketball in this town."

-Angelo Drossos

"When did I decide to start him? When I heard he could play for us. We're talking about the No. 4 scorer in the league. I'm not going to sit him on the bench."

-Tom Nissalke

"You don't stop George Gervin. You just hope that his arm gets tired after 40 shots. I believe the guy can score any time he wants to. I wonder if he gets bored out there."

-Dick Motta

"He's the one player I would pay to see play."

-Jerry West

"Gervin may be the best scorer I ever played against. You could do whatever you want, and it wouldn't matter."

-Quinn Buckner

"Gervin: Smooth as silk.....quick....great shot maker.....difficult to defend....it was a sight to see his spin shots."

-Rod Thorn

"Nobody in history scored points easier than Gervin. He would light you up and you didn't even know the match was lit. He had the efficiency and ability to be unstoppable."

-Steve Jones

George Gervin was a pioneer back in his day, the first of the tall shooting guards in the ABA/NBA. He was a unique player with a unique style, who created his own shot in almost any circumstance, making him one of the greatest shot-makers the NBA has ever seen. His release was lightening quick. A lot of Ice's shots looked like something out of a H-O-R-S-E game in your backyard. Whether he was facing a triple team or changing directions in midair,

15

Ice made seemingly impossible shots look as easy as free throws. Picture Manu Ginobili doing a trick shot in practice just for fun. Ice's shots seemed to be the same.........*except his shots were in games*. Ice could also run forever without losing a step, and he was truly one of the most explosive scorers that the NBA has ever seen. The faster the pace, the more he liked it. Even though it wasn't his signature shot, he had a 12 to 15-foot bank shot that was probably the most accurate of his era.

Ice's signature shot was the finger roll, which he is credited for inventing. He said he took a piece of the finger roll from Wilt Chamberlain, Julius Erving, and Connie Hawkins and made the shot famous. Ice said that he developed the shot because he got tired of dunking, and that the finger roll was smoother and easy for him to do with his long arms.

To Spurs fans, those 10 to 12-foot finger rolls were just as intriguing and entertaining as a Kareem Abdul-Jabbar sky hook. A lot of the players today use the finger roll to lay the ball up, but sometimes Ice used to finger roll from as far out as the free throw line. That shot is nowhere near as easy as it looks, especially from that distance. The amount of practice it takes to master the finger roll is mind-blowing.

In watching old games and highlight clips of Ice, I was amazed at how easy he made it all look. He seemed to defy his looks. How could somebody that thin dominate as easily as he was? Something just didn't seem to add up. Ice never looked like he was moving too fast or trying that hard, but he was a glider. The body control, attacks from all angles, the different ball spins off the glass, and the finger rolls made Ice an offensive machine. Ice didn't shoot a lot of 3-pointers because he believed it was the worst shot in the game. It's amazing that he shot 51% for his career and made it look so easy.

I remember watching a clip where Ice beat his man, the defense collapsed, he looked like he would do a reverse layup on the other side of the basket, but a defender closed and took away that option, so Ice - at the last second, in the air and under the basket, extended his arm toward the front of the rim and just flipped the ball up and in. All I could do was laugh out loud because that move was just flat out jaw-dropping and almost miraculous. On one other play, I saw him drive into the lane, get hit 3 or 4 times, spin, and do a finger roll from just in front of the free throw line and kiss it off the glass.........**UNBELIEVEABLE!!** When the Spurs needed a spark, you better believe that Ice would be taking over the game. No matter who was guarding him, no matter how much bigger, faster, or stronger the defender was, Ice was unstoppable.

4

The Ice Age

When George Gervin became a Spur, he was immediately put in the starting lineup by coach Tom Nissalke. He played his first game for the Spurs on February 7, 1974, which was an 86-83 loss to the Utah Stars. Ice shot 5-16 from the floor, scoring 12 points in his first start for the Spurs. He averaged 19.4 points in the Spurs' last 25 games of the 1973-74 regular season. That would prove to be a sample size of things to come. Ice, along with James Silas and Swen Nater gave the early Spurs teams a Big 3 of their own. Those 3 would lead the Spurs to a respectable 45-39 record, and a playoff berth. The Spurs drew the Pacers in the first round, losing to them in 7 games.

Bob Bass took over the Spurs' coaching reigns early in the 1974-75 season, bringing in a system that would take advantage of the Spurs' athletic talents. The key to the team's transformation was moving Ice from small forward to shooting guard. Coach Bass thought Ice would be more effective as a 6'7" shooting guard with a height advantage over the man guarding him instead of being lighter than every opponent at small forward. He also improved as a rebounder.

Ice had his best game against the Memphis Sounds on February 5, 1975, scoring 51 points in a 143-119 Spurs win. Ice didn't score in the 1st quarter, but he went on to get 25 points in the 2nd, 8 in the 3rd, and 18 in the 4th. These types of explosive games eventually became a common sight for anybody that watched Spurs games. The Spurs also improved to a 51-33 record that season, and finished 2nd in the ABA in scoring at 113.4 points per game.

The Spurs were still entertaining on the court in 1975-76, which was their last ABA season. It was their high-powered offense that made them attractive to the NBA, leading to them joining the league as a part of the merger despite not winning a playoff series in their first 3 years. The Spurs were led by James Silas, who was 6th in the league in scoring at 23.8 points per game, while Ice was 9th with 21.8. Once the Spurs made the jump to the NBA, they felt like they had something to prove. They wanted to show the fans that they belonged and they wanted to show the NBA players that they could compete.

The Iceman's career really started to take off in the 1976-77 season, which was the Spurs' first NBA season. Doug Moe was hired to coach the team after Bob Bass became the GM. Coach Moe wanted the Spurs to have the fastest offense in basketball. His benchmark for an offensive pace was a minimum of 100 shots per game. Ice credits Moe for making him into the player he became, and also says that Moe was his favorite coach.

Moe planned on starting the season with the same team he inherited from Coach Bass, but James Silas went down with a knee injury in the preseason and missed the first 60 games. George Karl, who was Silas' backup, was also out after having knee surgery. That left Mike Gale, who averaged 6.8 points off the bench in the previous season, with the starting point guard spot.

The Spurs opened that season up with a 121-118 win on the road against the Philadelphia 76ers on October 22, 1976. It turned out to be an up-and-down season for the Spurs, who lost 5 of their last 6 to finish with a 44-38 record, which was the 6th best in the league. The Spurs went on to get swept by the Boston Celtics in the 1st round of the playoffs. Ice finished 9th in the NBA in scoring with 23.1 points per game and shot .544 from the field, which is the 2nd best percentage in NBA history for a guard. The Spurs were the NBA's highest scoring team, averaging 115 points per contest. But their defense was ranked last in the league, giving up 114.4 per game.

The Spurs were led by Ice, Larry Kenon, and Billy Paultz in the 1977-78 season. They had several key injuries early in the year with Mike Gale, George Karl, and James Silas, but the team rebounded to finish 52-30 and clinch the Central Division. The Spurs went on to play the Washington Bullets in the first round of the 1978 playoffs. The Spurs were favored to win the series, but the Bullets pulled off the upset in 6 games. Ice averaged 33.2 points for the series, including a franchise playoff record of 46 points in Game 2.

The highlight of that season came on April 9, 1978, which was the last day of the regular season. George Gervin and Denver Nuggets shooting guard David Thompson, aka Skywalker, were in a tight race for the scoring title all season, and Ice won in a photo finish. Here's the story of that day in full:

When the last day of the regular season came around, both the Nuggets and the Spurs were locked into playoff spots and knew who they would be playing in the first round. That last regular season game was meaningless for both teams, who were going against non-playoff teams. The Nuggets played an afternoon game against the Pistons that day, and Skywalker scored 73 points to take the lead from Ice for the scoring title. The Nuggets beat the Pistons 139-137. At that time, that 73 points were the 3rd highest point total in league history. Only Wilt Chamberlain, with games of 100 in 1962 and 78 in 1961, had ever scored more points in a single game. That game boosted Skywalker's average to 27.15 points per game, slightly better than Ice, who was averaging 26.8.

The Spurs were in New Orleans later that night to play the Jazz. Before the game, Spurs coach Doug Moe instructed his players to get Ice the ball every time down the court, letting him take every shot until he had all the points he needed. Ice had led the NBA in scoring the whole season until that last game of the regular season, and to regain the scoring title, he needed 59 points. That would turn out to be a record-setting night for Ice, in more ways than one.

Ice missed his first 6 shots of the game, and then called a timeout and told his teammates to forget about the scoring title and just concentrate on winning the game. They ignored him, and he went on and scored 20 of the Spurs' 34 points in the 1st quarter. Ice got hot and scored 33 points in the 2nd quarter, breaking Skywalker's NBA record of 32 points in a quarter that he set earlier that day in his 73-point game. Ice was up to 53 points at halftime.

Early in the 3rd quarter, Ice hit a 10-foot jumper to score his 59th points, clinching the scoring title. Spurs athletic trainer John Anderson told Ice that he had all the points he needed, but Ice went back and scored 4 more points to take his total to a career-high 63 points. He said he wanted to score a few more points just in case the statisticians miscalculated. After clinching the scoring title, Ice sat for the rest of the 3rd and all of the 4th quarter. Those 63 points boosted his final scoring average to 27.22, beating out Skywalker (27.15) by the thinnest of margins.

The Iceman shot 23-49 from the floor and added 17 of 20 free throws to get his 63 points, all in just 33 minutes of play. Besides scoring 33 points in the 2nd quarter, he broke several other records. Ice tied the NBA record by making 12 field goals in the 2nd quarter. He broke his own Spurs single-game record of 51 points in a game. Ice also had stretches where he scored 22 and 18 consecutive points, breaking James Silas' previous Spurs record of 14. Ice also passed 10,000 career points (ABA/NBA combined) in that game, finishing with 10,014. In another milestone for the Spurs, Louie Dampier passed 15,000 career points, giving him 15,004. The Spurs lost to the Jazz 153-132.

Here are some interesting quotes from that night:

"It was incredible. They were throwing two and three guys at him, and he still hit 19 of 34 in the first half. The Jazz played him exclusively and let everybody else score."
　　　　　-(Spurs coach) Doug Moe

"I thought it might be easier for Ice to get 58 than for me to get two."
　　　　　-Louie Dampier

"He was great tonight. We tried to stop him but he was really tough, too tough."

-(Jazz coach) Elgin Baylor

After losing the 1978-79 season opener, the Spurs bounced back in a big way, spanking the Milwaukee Bucks 153-111 in the home opener. Once again, the Spurs led the NBA in scoring at 119.3 points per contest. The team also led the league in point differential, beating opponents by an average of 5.2 points. The Iceman led the league in scoring again, becoming the first guard in NBA history to win back-to-back scoring titles.

The Spurs were also bolstered by James Silas returning to the starting lineup after a 2-year absence because of knee surgery. At that point, the Spurs were 14-14, then went 34-20 for the rest of the season to finish 48-34. The Spurs won the Central Division for a 2nd straight year, finishing 1 game better than the Houston Rockets.

In the 1979 Eastern Conference Semifinals, the Spurs played the 76ers. The Spurs jumped out to a 2-0 series lead before the 76ers came back to tie the series at 3. The Spurs won Game 7 111-108 to take the series. Next for the Spurs were the Washington Bullets in the Eastern Conference Finals, which would be their best chance to win a championship. The Spurs won Games 1, 3, and 4 to go up 3-1 on the Bullets, putting them in the driver's seat. But the Bullets won the last 3 games by a total of 14 points: 4, 8, and 2. George Gervin averaged 28.6 points to lead all scorers in the playoffs.

Here's the story of the infamous Game 7 of the 1979 Eastern Conference Finals:

The Spurs were ahead by 10 points in the 4th quarter, but went cold in the final minutes. They missed 10 of 14 shots in that stretch. With 2:35 left in the game, the Spurs had possession and a 7-point lead. James Silas came off a screen set by Billy Paultz that sent Bullets guard Tom Henderson to the floor. Referee John Vanak called a moving violation on The Whopper. That questionable call was the turning point. At the other end, Bobby Dandridge hit a jumper over Larry

Kenon to cut the Spurs' lead down to 5.

With the game tied at 105, Dandridge made another jumper, this time a 12-footer from the right baseline with 8 seconds left to give the Bullets a 107-105 lead. James Silas' attempt to tie the game was blocked by Elvin Hayes, and the game was over. The Iceman scored 42 points, but was held scoreless in the last 3 minutes of the game. The Spurs became the 3rd team to ever blow a 3-1 series lead. The Spurs would have played the Seattle Supersonics in the NBA Finals, and it was believed that they would beat the Sonics because they had done so well against them in the regular season. The Iceman would never get that close to an NBA Finals again.

The 1979-80 season, which was the Spurs' last in the Eastern Conference, was a disappointing one for the team after winning the Central Division in the 2 seasons prior. The team finished with a 41-41 record and lost to the Rockets in the 1st round of the playoffs. Despite The Iceman lighting up the scoreboard and good seasons from James Silas and Larry Kenon, the Spurs hovered around the .500 mark all season. In January, Billy Paultz was traded to the Rockets for John Shumate, who contributed 14.7 points and 7.9 rebounds per game in his 27 games with the Spurs.

The Spurs were again the highest scoring team in the league at 119.4 points, but the team was hampered by a weak defense, which gave up 119.7 points per game. As a result, coach Doug Moe paid the price for the Spurs' sub-par season with his job. He was fired March 1 and replaced by Bob Bass as interim head coach. The Iceman was the bright spot for the Spurs that season. He won his 3rd straight scoring title by averaging a career-high 33.1 points per game, shooting 53% from the floor. Ice also led the NBA in field goals made (1,024) and attempted (1,940). A 34-point, 10-rebound performance in the 1980 NBA All-Star Game earned him the game's MVP award.

The Spurs would move to the Western Conference as a result of expansion and realignment before the 1980-81 season. The team joined the Rockets, (Kansas City) Kings, Nuggets, Jazz, and the expansion Dallas Mavericks in the Midwest Division. After the lackluster season the year before, the team made some key moves before the season. Stan Albeck was hired to coach the team after spending the previous season in Cleveland. In the 3 years he coached the Spurs they still scored in bunches, but they were much improved on defense. Also in those 3 years, the team averaged 51 wins and made the Western Conference Finals twice. After a holdout, Larry Kenon was traded to the Bulls on September 12, 1980 for cash and a couple of 1981 2nd round draft choices.

With the 15th pick in the 1980 NBA Draft, the Spurs took Reggie Johnson, a 6'9" power forward from Tennessee. In addition, Dave Corzine came over to the Spurs from the Bullets, and George Johnson was signed as a free agent. Those 3 frontcourt players combined with Mark Olberding, Kevin Restani, and Paul Griffin were known as the Bruise Brothers.

Here's some history on this nasty, intimidating frontcourt:

Once again, the Bruise Brothers nickname was given to the 6 big men that played for the Spurs in the early 1980s: Dave Corzine, Mark Olberding, George Johnson, Reggie Johnson, Kevin Restani, and Paul Griffin. Those 6 players introduced to San Antonio a new brand of basketball that was built on a blue collar work ethic, physical play, and hustle. They took pride in jarring the bones of opponents who tried to establish rebounding position in the paint. In December 1980, the Spurs gave away 10,000 free posters to fans the featured the Spurs' frontcourt as the Bruise Brothers. The nickname that was based on the hit movie, *The Blues Brothers*, which was released in June that same year.

The Bruise Brothers got teased by opposing players on the road about their nickname, but they were very serious about their role on the team. They led the NBA in rebounds, blocked shots, and were 3rd in personal fouls. George Johnson led the NBA in shot blocking with 3.4 blocks per game. Off the court they were too nice for their nickname. Here is a summary of their individual contributions from Spurs.com:

The Bruise Brothers hold a special place in Spurs history which makes it easy to forget that the group played together for a very short period of time ... after being 'born' during the 1980-81 season the group was broken up in the 1981-82 campaign (first Kevin Restani was waived on December 21, 1981, and, then, Reggie Johnson was traded on December 24) ... by the start of the 1982-83 season only member of the Bruise Brothers still on the Spurs roster was Paul Griffin ... here is a quick look at the six men who teamed together to make up the Bruise Brothers:

Mark Olberding (No. 53): Spent seven seasons in San Antonio ... selected by the Spurs, from San Diego, in the 1975 ABA Dispersal Draft ... traded to Chicago, along with Dave Corzine, on July 22, 1982 in exchange for Artis Gilmore ... played one ABA season and 11 NBA seasons ... was named to the 1975-76 ABA All-Rookie First Team ... hit 10-of-10 from the field, finishing with 22 points, in Boston on 1/21/77 ... enjoyed his best season in 1981-82 when he averaged 13.8 points and 6.5 rebounds for the Spurs.

Paul Griffin (No. 30): Played in San Antonio for four seasons ... was obtained by the Spurs on July 20, 1979, as compensation from Utah after the Jazz signed Allan Bristow ... retired following the 1982-83 season ... played seven NBA seasons ... averaged a career-best 6.3 points per game for the Spurs during the 1979-80 season.

Kevin Restani (No. 31): Spent two and a half seasons in San Antonio ... obtained from Milwaukee on August 31, 1979, for cash considerations ... waived by the Spurs on December 21, 1981 ... played eight NBA seasons ... during the 1979-80 campaign averaged a career-best 10.7 points per game ... inducted into the University of San Francisco Athletics Hall of Fame in 1985.

George Johnson (No. 52): Played two seasons with the Spurs ... signed by San Antonio as a free agent on August 15, 1980 ... traded to Atlanta in exchange for Jim Johnstone and a pair of second round draft picks on September 28, 1982 ... led the NBA in blocked shots three times in his 13-year career (1977-78, 1980-81 and 1981-82) ... holds the Spurs franchise record for the most blocks in a game with 13 vs. Golden State on 2/24/81 (in the game tied the NBA record for most blocks in a half with 11 in the second half) ... a member of the Golden State Warriors 1975 NBA Championship team.

Dave Corzine (No. 40): Spent two seasons in San Antonio ... obtained by the Spurs on September 26, 1980 from Washington in exchange for a pair of second round draft picks ... traded to Chicago, along with Mark Olberding, in exchange for Artis Gilmore on July 22, 1982 ... spent seven of his 13 NBA seasons with the Bulls ... one of the top players in DePaul history: ranks third on the school's all-time scoring list and is the Blue Demons all-time rebounding leader.

Reggie Johnson (No. 32): With the Spurs for just one and a half seasons ... selected by San Antonio in the first round of the 1980 NBA Draft, with the 15th overall pick ... traded to Cleveland, along with Ron Brewer, in exchange for Mike Mitchell and Roger Phegley on December 24, 1981 ... played four seasons in the NBA ... won an NBA Championship in 1983 with the Philadelphia 76ers ... in 2009 was one of 20 men named to University of Tennessee's All-Century Team.

The Spurs got off to a 10-2 start to the 1980-81 season. They ended the season with a 52-30 record, winning the Midwest Division for the 3rd division title in 4 years. The team was upset by the Rockets in the 1st round, coming up short in 7 games. Halfway through the season, the Spurs made an important acquisition, trading Ron Brewer and George Johnson to the Cavaliers for Mike Mitchell, who would average 21 points a night in his first year with the Spurs. In the offseason, the Spurs traded James Silas to the Cavaliers. He was the last Spur on the team left from the Dallas Chaparrals days. The emergence of Johnny Moore made the trade possible.

The Spurs' offense was a major factor in a successful 1981-82 season. On March 6, 1982, the Spurs beat the Bucks in triple overtime 171-166, led by George Gervin's 50 points. That 337 points from the Spurs and Bucks is the 2nd highest point total in NBA history behind the Pistons and Nuggets, who combined for 370 points on December 13, 1983. The Spurs finished the season ranked 3rd in the NBA in scoring at 113.1 points per game behind the Nuggets (126.5) and Lakers (114.6). After finishing 3rd in scoring behind Adrian Dantley (30.7) and Moses Malone (27.8) in the previous season, The Iceman came back to win his 4th and final NBA scoring title with 32.3 points per game. The Spurs also had another league leader in Johnny Moore, who emerged to take over as the team's starting point guard. He led the NBA in assists with 9.6 per game.

The Spurs finished the season with a 48-34 record, claiming a 2nd straight Midwest Division title. They went on to play the SuperSonics in the 1st round of the playoffs, splitting the first 2 games, then winning 3 straight close games to take the series. The Spurs moved to play the Lakers in the Western Conference Finals, only to get swept by them on their way to a championship. The Spurs made another key acquisition in the offseason, trading Mark Olberding and Dave Corzine to the Bulls for Artis Gilmore. One other notable move the Spurs made was acquiring Mike Dunleavy, Sr. as a free agent.

The Spurs won their 3rd consecutive Midwest Division title by finishing with a 53-29 record for the 1982-83 season. The 53 wins was a franchise record at that time. The Spurs made it happen with excellent all-around play. The team was 2nd in the NBA in scoring, rebounding, blocked shots, and assists. George Gervin finished 4th in scoring with 26.2 points per game. Artis Gilmore proved to be an excellent fit on the Spurs, having another All-Star season. The A-Train averaged 18 points, 12 rebounds, and 2.3 blocks, and his .626 field goal percentage led the NBA. Mike Mitchell, in his first full season with the Spurs, averaged 19.9 points and 6.7 rebounds. Johnny Moore was 2nd in the league in assists with 9.8 per game.

The Spurs squared off with the Nuggets in the Western Conference Semifinals, with the Spurs winning Game 1 by a score of 152-133. That was a new single-game postseason record for total points. The Spurs capped the series off in 5 games, winning the closeout game 145-105. The Spurs averaged 132.8 points for the series to the Nuggets' 119.4. The Conference Finals was a rematch with the Lakers. The Spurs were swept by the Lakers in 1982, but this time they put up a better fight. The Spurs took the Lakers to 6 games before losing 101-100 in Game 6.

After winning their division in 5 of the previous 6 seasons, the bottom fell out on the Spurs in the 1983-84 season. The team's problems started in the offseason when Stan Albeck left to take the head coaching job with the New Jersey Nets. Morris McHone, who served as an assistant for 4 years under Albeck, took over as his replacement. McHone would only coach 31 games, posting an 11-20 record. He was fired before the new year. GM Bob Bass stepped in and tried to restore order, but didn't have much luck.

In a December 17 loss to the Atlanta Hawks, George Gervin was held to 8 points, breaking his streak of 407 straight games of scoring in double figures. Artis Gilmore and Johnny Moore spent good chunks of the season on the injured list, and the Spurs lost 14 of 18 games after the All-Star break. Despite winning 5 out of their last 7 games to end the season, the Spurs finished with a 37-45 record, missing the playoffs.

There were several bright spots for the Spurs in a season that was otherwise lackluster. The Iceman had his 7th consecutive (and final) season of averaging at least 25 points per game, with 25.9 per game. The A-Train led the NBA in field goal percentage (.631) for the 2nd consecutive year. John Lucas, who came to the Spurs in December from the Continental Basketball Association, finished 4th in the league with 10.7 assists. In the last game of the regular season, which was a 157-154 loss to the Nuggets, Lucas set an NBA record with 14 assists in a quarter and a team record with 24 assists in a game. Johnny Moore finished 5th in the NBA in assists, with behind Lucas at 9.6 per game. On February 28, 1984, James Silas became the first Spurs player to have his jersey retired.

The Spurs hired Cotton Fitzsimmons in the offseason to rebuild the team. Early on he looked to be in the running for the Coach Of The Year award, leading the Spurs to a 5-1 start to the 1984-85 season. Soon after that nice start, the team had a 7-game losing streak and struggled to play .500 basketball the rest of the season. The Spurs finished the season with a 41-41 record. They almost pulled off the upset against the Nuggets in the 1st round, pushing them to the limit before getting blown out in Game 5. The team didn't even have a winning month until they went 8-5 in January. The highlight of that month was the 139-94 win over the Golden State Warriors on January 8 in which Johnny Moore missed a quadruple-double by a single steal. His stat line that night was 26 points, 13 assists, 11 rebounds, and 9 steals. Mike Mitchell was the Spurs' leading scorer that season with 22.2 points per game. George Gervin, who was in his last season with the Spurs, was 2nd with 21.2 points.

5
Ice By The Numbers

Here is George Gervin by the numbers (taken from Spurs.com):

4 – Ice won four NBA scoring titles during his 10-year NBA career … Michael Jordan (10), Wilt Chamberlain (7), Allen Iverson (4), and Kevin Durant (4) are the only four other players in NBA history to have four or more scoring titles.

9 – Gervin was named to the All-NBA/ABA team nine times … Gervin earned All-NBA First Team honors five times (1978, '79, '80, '81 and '82) … he was named to the All-NBA Second Team in 1977 and 1983 … he garnered All-ABA second team honors in 1975 and 1976.

12 – Ice appeared in 12 All-Star games (9 NBA and 3 ABA) … he won the All-Star MVP Award in 1980 … just one of 23 players to be named an All-Star 12 or more times.

26.3 – Gervin's scoring average (NBA/ABA combined) in his 12 seasons with the Silver and Black … the Iceman averaged 22.2 ppg in three ABA seasons and bumped that average up to 27.3 ppg in his nine NBA seasons in San Antonio …

for his career Gervin averaged 25.1 ppg (NBA/ABA combined) which ranks 11th all-time … his 26.2 ppg scoring average in NBA games only ranks eighth all-time.

33 – On April, 9, 1978 at New Orleans, Gervin exploded for 33 second-quarter points en route to his first scoring title … the 33 points stood as the most points scored in a quarter in NBA history until Klay Thompson scored 37 points in the third quarter on January 23, 2015 against the Sacramento Kings.

44 – The number Gervin wore during his 12 seasons with the Spurs … his jersey was retired on December 5, 1987, and is just one of six jerseys that hangs from the rafters of the AT&T Center.

53 – Had a streak of 53 straight games with 20 or more points.

63 – On April, 9, 1978 at New Orleans, in the final game of the 1977-78 season, Gervin was in a battle with David Thompson for the league's scoring title … Thompson had scored 73 earlier in the day and appeared to have claimed the title … Gervin knew he had to score 58 points to edge out Thompson and he came through… Ice had 53 at halftime and finished the game with 63 points -despite sitting out the fourth quarter- to claim his first scoring title … Head Coach Doug Moe said, "We let him have the chance to do it, but nobody else could have done it. New Orleans put three guys on him and didn't even guard a couple of our guys! And, he still scored! He put on one of the most amazing shows I have ever seen."

407 – Gervin recorded a remarkable streak of 407 consecutive games scoring in double figures

.510 – Gervins's shooting percentage during his 12 years (NBA/ABA combined) with the Silver and Black … Iceman connected on 9,170 of his 17,993 field goals during his career.

899 – The number of games Ice played in a Spurs uniform … Gervin played in

190 ABA games from 1974-76 and saw action in 709 NBA games for the Silver and Black ... he ranks third on the Spurs all-time NBA/ABA games list and fourth in NBA games only.

2,585 – Gervin scored 2,585 points during the 1979-80 season to win the second of his four NBA Scoring Titles ... for the year the Iceman averaged 33.1 points.

19,383 – The number of NBA points Gervin scored with the Silver and Black ... ranks third on the Spurs all-time NBA points scored list ... for his career Ice scored 20,708 NBA points which ranks 34th in NBA history ... he is just one of 37 players to score 20,000 or more points during their NBA career.

23,602 – The combined NBA/ABA points Ice scored in his 12 years with the Spurs, which ranks first on the Spurs all-time NBA/ABA points scored ... for his career Gervin scored 26,595 combined points which ranks 14th in NBA/ABA history.

6

Influence On The Game

Just how good was George Gervin? Let me start by stating the obvious: He is **HANDS DOWN** a top 5 shooting guard of all-time. He is also the most efficient scoring guard in NBA history. He was the epitome of the title "pure scorer", but he rarely gets mentioned in discussions of the greatest scorers of all time. Ice wasn't a gunner. He was big on quality more than volume, and his career shooting percentage (51%) is proof that he hardly ever took a bad shot. As a lifetime 25.1 points per game scorer, Ice just knew what to do with the basketball and how to do it.

I also believe that Ice is tragically underrated, for 2 main reasons:

1.) His accomplishments get discredited because of the era he played in.

There has been talk over the years that the reason Ice's numbers are so big is because he played in the era where scoring was at its highest. In other words, he has been trivialized and labeled as a product of his era. Ice's numbers were gaudy even when he played, not just by today's standards. Those numbers also went hand in hand with winning as the Spurs' franchise player. And Ice didn't just score. He scored the best, or among the best, in the NBA while shooting 51% for his entire career. That percentage is amazing for a 6'7" guard that didn't live under the basket. As a matter of fact, 50% has long been the line of demarcation between elite and very good shooters. That's not all there is to it, but being over 50% while being an elite scorer definitely qualifies The Iceman as one of the great scorers in NBA history.

Let me take it a step further: How many shooting guards have scored more than Ice while shooting over 50% for their careers? The answer is.........**ZERO!!** If shooting 50% is as easy as Ice's detractors claim, why was it just as uncommon in his era as it is now? These naysayers have also said that Ice's 4 scoring titles came easy to him. Let me first point out that no other guard had led the NBA in scoring as many times as he did before Michael Jordan came along. If winning scoring titles is that easy, how come only 4 other players in NBA history have won 4 or more? All of those players have spent their whole pro careers in the NBA unlike The Iceman, who spent 4 years in the ABA.

Michael Jordan (10) and Wilt Chamberlain (7) are the only 2 players that have won more scoring titles than Ice. This quote from MJ speaks volumes: ***"George told me he did it by trying to score 4 baskets per quarter."*** That was him crediting Ice with teaching him how to win scoring titles. Keep in mind that MJ won 10 of those. That should give some perspective on the impact Ice has had on the NBA. Again, winning multiple scoring titles shooting over 50% *as a shooting guard* is noteworthy and extremely uncommon. It's a far cry from being "just a scorer". That's more like being "the scorer" before MJ and remaining "the other scorer" aside from MJ to this day, which brings me to a point I would like to reemphasize: **George Gervin is the most efficient guard in NBA history.....***regardless of era and how easy points were to come by in it.***

2.) As the most efficient scoring guard in NBA history, he gets labeled as doing nothing but scoring.

The Iceman gets a bad rap for the defense he played in his career, especially from the media. There was the misconception that the Spurs didn't care much about defense, only that he outscored whoever was guarding Ice. Anybody that thinks all he did was score has missed the bigger picture. I see it a different way. There was less defense in the NBA in general in his era, the refs called the games much tighter back then, and the Spurs didn't want Ice to get in foul trouble.

The Iceman was actually a pretty good rebounder, he could come up with steals, and he was an exceptional shot blocker at his position. His rebounding numbers were higher than any guard or small forward the Spurs have had besides Alvin Robertson until Kawhi Leonard became a Spur. Ice also did a good job at defending the passing lanes and on help defense, averaging 1.3 steals and 1 block per game for his career.

When he retired, Ice had the most blocks by a guard in NBA history. Did you know that in 1979 he became the first Spur to record a 5x5 game? In that game he had 21 points, 5 rebounds, 6 assists, 5 blocks, and 5 steals. You don't have monster games like that without playing defense. Here's one more interesting fact regarding Ice's defense: **He was the first guard in NBA history to have 100 blocks and 100 steals in the same season.** In fact, he did it 5 times in his career if you include his ABA years. Ice was also the first guard to average 25+ points while posting the 100/100 line.

The last 2 guards to lead the NBA in scoring have been Dwyane Wade and Russell Westbrook. You could talk all day long about how those 2 would average 35 points or more back in the 80's, but that might not be entirely accurate. Keep in mind that the NBA had 6 to 8 fewer teams than the current NBA. That means teams back then were much deeper than they are now. When George Gervin was winning his scoring titles, there were teams that had Hall Of Famers coming off their benches. On top of that, the European players hadn't started influencing the league yet, so the game was much more physical back then.

The Iceman was a 1st Team All-NBA player for 5 consecutive seasons (1978-1982), another accomplishment that cuts across generations. The only other Spur to have that many 1st Team selections is Tim Duncan, who has 10. Ice also had a couple of 2nd Team selections sandwiched around those 5 seasons on the 1st Team. A lot of naysayers use the excuse, "I never saw him play" as a rationale to trivialize The Iceman's accomplishments and his place in NBA history. When it comes to the criteria used in subjective discussions like this one - major statistical categories, longevity, team success, the player's role in that success, influence in the sport, I don't see how you can look at all of those things and come up with a justification for downplaying or underselling what Ice has done in his career. Just because you can't remember what he accomplished because you either weren't born yet or too young to remember doesn't trivialize what the man did.

One other noteworthy accomplishment for George Gervin was him being in the top 11 in MVP voting every season from 1976-77 through 1982-83, basically his whole prime. He was 11th in 1977, 2nd in 1978 and 1979, 3rd in 1980, and 9th in 1983. No disrespect to Bill Walton, who won the 1978 MVP, but I believe Ice got snubbed. Here's how it went down:

Bill Walton, who was one of the dominant centers in the NBA at that time, had the best season of his career. He averaged 18.9 points, 13.2 rebounds, 5 assists, and 2.5 blocks per game to go with 52% shooting. Big Red was an unselfish big man who made teammates better, one of the all-time great passing centers. It also didn't hurt that he was already a reigning champion. Even though he only played 58 games in the 1977-78 season, the case for Bill Walton winning the MVP was this: The Blazers went 50-10 in their first 60 games. He missed the last 22 regular season games after breaking his foot while the Blazers limped to an 8-14 finish, but they *still* finished with a league-high 58 wins and home court advantage for the playoffs. That's what ultimately swayed the voters. In a nutshell, Big Red missed 24 games and had a HUGE impact on the regular season. The Blazers won 50 games with him in the lineup, in a season where only 2 other teams won 50 wins.....the 76ers (55) and Spurs (52).

George Gervin averaged 27.2 points, 5.1 rebounds, 3.7 assists, 1.7 steals, and 1.3 blocks per game. He shot 54% from the floor and 83% from the free throw line, and did all of that in just under 35 minutes per game while winning his first scoring title and leading the Spurs to 52 wins. I don't question Bill Walton's dominance during that season or his dominance in leading the Blazers to a championship in the previous season, I just can't see anybody qualifying for MVP to a player that missed a third of the season when the NBA's leading scorer was a well-deserving candidate. At the end of the day, the MVP voters felt like none of the runners-up made a strong enough case for their choice to be called into question.

One other aspect of George Gervin's game that was underrated was his competitiveness. His coolness on the court made it seem like he wasn't playing hard, but he was **ALWAYS** a competitor and always rose to the challenge. That April 9, 1978 Jazz game is a good example of that, even though the Spurs didn't win. Think about it for a second. First of all, that game was in New Orleans, not the friendly confines of San Antonio. That meant both Ice and the entire New Orleans Jazz team knew he needed 59 points to win the scoring title. Then he went out and scored 63 in a hostile environment. I can't think of one player today that has that kind of "on/off switch". How many players could need 59 points in a specific game, with everybody in the building aware of it, and then go out and get it done? Even Jazz coach Elgin Baylor was impressed with that effort. This is a man who had games of 71, 65, and 64 points himself as a player.

From a historical perspective, the late 70's/early 80's Spurs might be the best forgotten team in NBA history. When it comes to judging The Iceman's place in history, he often gets penalized for never making it to the NBA Finals. It's not like the Spurs flamed out in the 1st round every year. Ice was the main reason they didn't. They didn't make it to the Finals, but they still played in 3 Conference Finals in a 5-year period, something that the Spurs franchise has done only 2 other times. They did it in 1999-2001-2003, and the other stretch was recent. Within these last 5 years, the Spurs have played in 3 consecutive Western Conference Finals with back-to-back NBA Finals trips. The playoffs in the George Gervin Era were select company. As competitive as the NBA was back then, even making it out of the 1st round meant something. Either way, those Spurs team in that era were among the NBA's final 4 teams in multiple seasons. The Iceman was a major reason for that happening.

The Iceman's Influence On The Game

George Gervin was a game-changer, somebody that's had an impact on the NBA well after his last hoop. He made the finger roll famous and showed everybody many different ways to put the ball in the basket. Before Ice came along, shooting was just a basic execution. The jump shot was the game's standard for scoring. Ice added unique and lasting flair to what were once routine shots. Before him, the NBA had Elgin Baylor and Earl Monroe who were creative in their own right, but they were masters at body control. The Iceman came around and mastered the finger control. He was the first one to put an emphasis on "spin", the art of releasing the ball with enough twist of the fingers to make it do crazy things.

Ice's shots ricocheted off the glass from impossible angles and fell through the net. He released his shot either with his fingers under the ball or over it, putting a different spin on it whenever he wanted to. Depending on how tall Ice's defender was, his trajectory was high or low. He had a wide variety of moves in his arsenal. In basketball today, just about everybody knows how to finger roll or drive into the lane and drop a runner. These shots have become requirements for any player wanting to specialize in scoring, and taken for granted because they are so common.

One other aspect of Ice's influence that gets overlooked was the increase in size for the prototypical shooting guard. Before him, the standard height for that position was 6'3". That was the case through the late 70's/early 80's. At 6'7", Ice was too big for the guards in his era to handle on the interior. In the late 70's, after Ice had been dominating his competition for a few years, other teams started either converting their small forward into shooting guards or drafting bigger 2-guards. It started with the Suns and Walter Davis, then came guys like Rolando Blackman, Clyde Drexler, Michael Jordan, Kobe Bryant, and Tracy McGrady. By the way, the latter 3 have all won scoring titles.

George Gervin's style and charisma were instrumental in introducing pro basketball to a city that was previously a high school football town. He and James Silas were the team's undisputed stars, but it was Ice that gave the team its identity. He put San Antonio on the basketball map. It's interesting to think about what might have happened to the Spurs if that deal for Ice had been blocked and he was forced to go back to Virginia. It's hard to say, but they most definitely would have been deprived of their first superstar. David Robinson is still the most beloved player in Spurs history, and Tim Duncan changed the fortunes of the franchise. But without Ice being there to lay the foundation, San Antonio probably wouldn't have ever gotten to enjoy either one of them. The Iceman might be the most recognizable landmark of San Antonio outside of the Alamo and the Riverwalk. Despite not bringing a championship to the city, Ice is just as beloved as the Spurs' other 2 franchise players.

After 12 seasons with the Spurs George Gervin was traded to the Bulls, where he played the 1985-86 season, his last in the NBA. Ice averaged 16.2

points per game in Chicago. He played the 1986-87 season for Banco Roma in Italy, averaging 26.1 points for the season. Ice retired briefly before making a comeback in the Continental Basketball Association with the Quad City Thunder, averaging 20.3 points in 14 games for them in 1989.

His last stop would be in Spain to play the 1989-90 season for TDK Manresa, before retiring for good. Ice averaged 25.5 points for that season, and had 31 points and 15 rebounds in his last pro basketball game. He was later hired by the Spurs as a community relations representative, a position that he held until 1992, when head coach and former teammate John Lucas made him an assistant coach. After 2 seasons on the bench, Ice returned to his position in the community relations department in 1994, which is his current position. Ice also had a brief stint as a head coach in the new ABA with the Detroit Dogs, with help from his son (point guard) George, Jr., leading them to the league's first championship at the end of the 2000-01 season.

Since he retired from basketball, The Iceman has played an even bigger role in the community than he did with the Spurs. He never stopped giving back to the community that made him a people's champion. He has a strong motivation to give back because he was a product of being an underprivileged kid. Along with the George Gervin Academy, Ice has several organizations for kids that need them, including a house for teenage girls coping with difficult pregnancies. He also participates in basketball clinics. In this sense, he has topped anything he ever contributed as an athlete.

I believe a big part of why The Iceman is underappreciated is because are so many younger Spurs fans that didn't get to see him play. If you didn't get to see a player play, especially in his prime, it's hard to have a true understanding of that player's impact on the game. I'm talking about myself too, because I didn't get to see Ice play. I didn't really see the impact he had on basketball until I started doing my research for this book. It was only fitting that he became the first Spur to be elected into the Basketball Hall Of Fame in 1996. His place among the NBA's 50 Greatest is also well-deserved. If you ask me, I think he should be somewhere in the top half of those 50 players. After realizing Ice's impact and putting some things in perspective, I appreciate him and his contributions so much more than I already did.

7

The Iceman's Best Teammates

Those George Gervin-led Spurs teams really were some quality teams. Even though they didn't win a championship, they still made it to the playoffs 11 times, including 3 trips to the Conference Finals. At the end of the day, those teams were competitive , as well as entertaining. If they couldn't do anything else, they could definitely put the ball in the basket. Here is a look at The Iceman's best teammates with the Spurs:

James Silas

-2x ABA All-Star (1975-1976)
-All-ABA First Team (1976)
-All-ABA Second Team (1975)
-ABA All-Rookie First Team (1973)
-ABA All-Time Team
-#13 Retired (Spurs)

James Silas was drafted in the 5th round of the 1972 NBA Draft (70th overall) by the Houston Rockets. He never played a game for them because he was released before the 1972-73 season even started. After Silas cleared waivers by the NBA, he signed with the Dallas Chaparrals in late November. He would develop into a standout. Here are some quotes that speak to how great

James Silas was and his contribution to the Spurs:

"He had an uncanny ability to control the tempo of a basketball game, and a competitive ferocity that inspired a struggling ABA franchise after it moved from Dallas to San Antonio in 1973."

-David Flores (former SA Express-News columnist)

"The image of James Silas going up high and taking that jump shot late in a game is not a memory that's easily erased. It was uncanny how he could deliver that shot. He could jump so high and his shot was so pretty."

-Terry Stembridge (former Spurs broadcaster)

"Ice would take what the other team gave him, but Jimmy Si would take what he wanted. He had a burning desire to win and a huge, huge heart."

-Coby Dietrick

"You know, it's no mistake that this jersey is up there next to mine. We both brought national attention to San Antonio."

"James Silas is definitely one of the lost guys who doesn't get the credit he deserves, especially for playing the one spot. I would do all the damage during three quarters and in the fourth quarter we'd get him the ball because we knew he was 'Captain Late.' The things that he could do to those little point guards was amazing. Plus, he never really missed a free throw."

-George Gervin

Before George Gervin became a Spur the team was led by James Silas, a point guard out of Stephen F. Austin University. The 6'1", 185-pound guard was a 2-time All-American in college. He was nicknamed Captain Late by Spurs broadcaster Terry Stembridge because of his clutchness late in the game and his ability to routinely produce 20-point 4th quarter performances. His teammates knew him as unselfish and a fierce competitor, and it's been said that he was the best leader to ever play for the Spurs. Captain Late consistently delivered in late game situations, even if the intention wasn't to go in his direction, the ball often still ended up in his hands.

Captain Late developed his game by watching techniques and moves used by other players. He paid special attention to players who could penetrate, take a hit, and get the shot off. He strongly believed in taking the shot he wanted instead of what the defense gave him. Captain Late was uncommonly strong for his size and had excellent leaping ability for his size, able to touch the top of the square in the middle of the backboard. He was also a master at putting an opponent at his mercy and making the defender touch him in ways that if they were both moving, he would draw the foul and still get the shot off most of the time.

When Bob Bass took over as Spurs head coach in 1974-75, he moved The Iceman to shooting guard to play next to Captain Late. With them together, the Spurs had the best backcourt in the ABA. It was also believed that they were the best guard tandem in all of basketball, including the Knicks' pairing of Walt Frazier and Earl Monroe. Captain Late embraced pressure so much that Ice deferred to him in the 4th quarter because of his ability to get to the free throw line. In fact, he ranked in the top 10 in free throw percentage in 6 separate seasons, shooting 85.5% for his career.

The Spurs built a lot of their offense around Captain Late's ability to break down opposing defenses late in the game. He had the ability to back his opponents down, and if you came to double, the Spurs had the floor spaced well enough for him to either make the pass or make the shot and get fouled. The release on Captain Late's jump shot was so high that nobody could block it. After backing his man down, he would shoot a little fall away that was almost impossible to guard if you didn't double him.

Captain Late played 8 seasons (9 if you include the season with the Chaps), including 5 years in the NBA after the Spurs entered the league in 1976. His best seasons were the ones from when the team was still in the ABA. His best season turned out to be the 1975-76 season. Here's a look at Captain Late at his best:

His best season was the 1975-76 season, which was the Spurs' final ABA season. He averaged 23.8 points (6th in the ABA), 5.4 assists (5th), 4 rebounds, and 1.8 steals (9th). Captain Late also finished 4th in field goal percentage

(.519), 4th in free throw percentage (.872), and 5th in minutes played (3,112). He also made the All-ABA First Team. A completely dominant season from Dr. J is the only thing that kept him from winning the MVP. That season was ruined for Captain Late when he broke his ankle landing on the foot of Nets guard Brian Taylor after shooting a jump shot in Game 1 of the ABA semifinals. The Nets went on to beat the Spurs and claim the last ABA championship.

James Silas completely recovered from his broken ankle in time for the 1976-77 season, the Spurs' first in the NBA. The Spurs were supposed to be contenders that year, but their title hopes vanished when Captain Late blew out his knee when he collided with Bill Robinzine of the Kings in a preseason game. With a healthy James Silas, there is no question that the Spurs would have had a better record than 44-38. They also would have been a more dangerous matchup for the Celtics in the playoffs. Captain Late was limited to 59 games out of a possible 164 over the next 2 seasons. Even though he managed to stay healthy for the rest of his career, he was never the same player he was in the ABA. He never averaged more than 18 points a game from that point on.

Here are couple of quotes from Bob Bass describing how the injury changed James Silas' game:

"He just wasn't as explosive. (Before the injury) he could really elevate when he penetrated. When he drove to the basket he could take a hit and finish the shot as well as anybody I've ever seen--maybe the best I've ever seen. You could hit him and he was so strong and could elevate so high that he could still finish the shot. He was a great free throw shooter. It's amazing—George Gervin led the NBA in scoring four times, but he never got to the free throw line as much you'd think he would. He had all of these tricks; he'd move under you or over you. But James Silas could draw a foul as well as anybody who ever played."

"My recollections of when he was really great are from before he got hurt, when he was playing against us. He was absolutely the best—the ultimate guy at the end of the game. He was just terrific. Unfortunately, he hurt his knee and was never quite the same—still a great player, but there is no

telling how great he would have been had he not gotten hurt. People really didn't get to know the real Silas in the NBA. That is a shame. He really was 'Captain Late' and he was the best."

James Silas played 3,000+ minutes in the 3 seasons before his catastrophic knee injury, but only 667 over the next 2 seasons. He would never again play more than 2,300 minutes. By the 1978-79 season, he was healthy enough to play a full season. The Spurs got a big boost when Captain Late got back in the starting lineup, going on to finish with a 48-34 record, which was the 2nd best in the Eastern Conference. He averaged 16 points and 3.5 assists in the regular season, and bumped those numbers up to 19.1 and 4.7 in the playoffs. Captain Late's numbers improved to 17.7 points and 4.5 assists in 1979-80. In 1980-81, his last season as a Spur, he put up 17.7 points and 3.8 assists.

After the 1980-81 season, James Silas was traded to the Cleveland Cavaliers for a 2nd-round draft choice and cash. He played 67 games and averaged 11.2 points, 3.3 assists, 1.6 rebounds, and 0.6 steals per game. After 10 years of pro basketball, Captain Late's career averages are 16.1 points, 3.8 assists, 3 rebounds, and 1 steal per game. He shot .495 from the field and .855 from the free throw line. On April 15, 1983, Captain Late was selected to the Spurs' All-Decade Team, along with George Gervin, Artis Gilmore, Mike Mitchell, and Mark Olberding. On February 28, 1984 he became the first Spur to have his number retired for his many great contributions to the team. The early history of the Spurs franchise is impossible to analyze without highlighting James Silas, who also happens to be one of the more underrated players in pro basketball history.

Artis Gilmore

-Consensus First Team All-American (1971)

-ABA Rookie Of The Year (1972)

-ABA MVP (1972)

-ABA All-Rookie First Team (1972)

-ABA Champion (1975)

-ABA Playoffs MVP (1975)

-5x ABA All-Star (1972-1976)

-ABA All-Star Game MVP (1974)

-5x All ABA First Team (1972-1976)

-4x ABA All-Defensive First Team (1973-1976)

-ABA All-Time Team

-6x NBA All-Star (1978-1979, 1981-1983, 1986)

-NBA All-Defensive Second Team (1978)

-Basketball Hall Of Fame (2011)

Artis Gilmore was the man who solidified the center position for the Spurs from 1982-1987. Before he became a Spur, he was already a well-accomplished player. After playing 2 years of junior college basketball, The A-Train went on to play at Jacksonville University, where he was an All-American. At Jacksonville, he became one of only 5 college players to ever average at least 20 points and 20 rebounds over his career. The A-Train led the nation in rebounding as a junior and senior, and his career average of 22.7 rebounds is still the highest in NCAA Division I history.

The A-Train started his pro career with the ABA's Kentucky Colonels. Right away, he was so dominant that he earned the rare distinction of being named both Rookie Of The Year and MVP of the 1971-72 season. He would be a star as long as the ABA lasted. In his 5 years in that league, the A-Train led the ABA in rebounding 4 times, twice in blocks per game and field goal percentage, and once in personal fouls. He also finished in the top 10 in scoring all 5 seasons and set ABA records for career blocks (750), blocks during a season (422 in 1971-72), career field goal percentage (.557), and rebounds in one game (40 vs the Nets, 2/3/74). The A-Train was named to the All-ABA First Team in all 5 of his ABA seasons, and the All-Defensive Team 4 times. He also played in the All-Star Game in all 5 of his ABA seasons, earning the MVP in 1974. The highlight of his ABA career was leading the Colonels to a 1975 championship and being named MVP of the playoffs that season.

When the ABA folded in 1976, The A-Train was picked first overall by the Chicago Bulls in the 1976 ABA Dispersal Draft. Most of his time as a Bull was unpleasant, with them only making the playoffs twice and the A-Train feeling unappreciated. He averaged a double-double and made the All-Star team all 6 of his years in Chicago. He consistently ranked near the top of the NBA in rebounds, blocks, and field goal percentage. His .670 field goal percentage in 1980-81 is the 3rd highest of all time, with the top 2 spots belonging to Wilt Chamberlain. The A-Train was just as reliable as he was in his ABA years, playing in 250 straight games for the Bulls before he suffered a knee injury early in the 1979-80 season. He came back to play in 212 straight games.

After the 1981-82 season, the A-Train was traded to the Spurs for Dave Corzine, Mark Olberding, and cash. He left the Bulls as their 3rd leading rebounder and 4th leading scorer all-time, and as the center who played Kareem Abdul-Jabbar the toughest of any center in the NBA. In his 5 seasons with the Spurs, the A-Train shot 62% from the floor, which is still a Spurs record. They were already a good team when he got there, and he fit right in after many thought he was too old to contribute. The 1982-83 season was the A-Train's best season with the Spurs. He averaged 18 points, 12 rebounds, and 2.3 blocks. He also led the NBA in field goal percentage for the 3rd straight season and earned another All-Star selection.

Over a 3-game stretch in March of that season, The A-Train put up 96 points and 35 rebounds. He helped lead the Spurs to a 53-29 record, which was the best in Spurs history to that point. Best of all, The A-Train got the appreciation he was looking for, especially from George Gervin. Here's a quote from Ice to sum it up: *"I love it. I have never played with a dominant center before, and I'm enjoying it."* In the following years, Ice kept scoring and The A-Train kept on doing his thing: intimidating, rebounding, and blocking shots, and shooting with record precision. He was among the top 2 in field goal percentage in all 5 of his seasons with the Spurs. The A-Train played his last All-Star Game in 1985-86, at age 36. The Spurs finished last in the division that season. As a team on the decline, they won between 28 and 41 games a year in The A-Train's last 4 seasons on the team and made the playoffs twice, losing in the first round twice.

After his output had been reduced to 11.4 points and 7.1 rebounds per game, The A-Train was sent back to the Bulls for a 2nd round pick. He would only play 24 games for them in 1987-88 before being released. The Celtics picked up The A-Train, and he finished the season as a backup to Robert Parish before retiring that summer at age 38. He left the NBA with 15,579 points, 9161 rebounds, 1747 blocks, and an NBA record .599 career shooting percentage. A year after retiring, The A-Train made a comeback with Bologna Arimo of the Italian League in 1988-89. The A-Train averaged 12.3 points and 11 rebounds for them and made the European All-Star Team.

Artis Gilmore's basketball career went largely underappreciated for a very long time. A major factor in that was his ABA years being so heavily discounted, which is why it took so long for him to get into the Basketball Hall Of Fame. At 7'2", 250 pounds, he is regarded as the strongest man to ever play in the NBA next to Wilt Chamberlain. That super strength, combined with great timing, incredible athleticism, and being left-handed made him an intimidating presence and unstoppable force. Few big men left the kind of mark The A-Train left on all levels of basketball- college, ABA, and NBA. He was an all-around A-level player, but his Hall candidacy unfairly fell short over the years.

Along with not getting enough credit for his 5 years in the ABA, The A-Train was also penalized by the voters for being on mediocre NBA teams that didn't contend for championships. The door open for The A-Train to get into the Hall when they created an ABA committee to recognize overlooked ABA players like him. There is no way that Artis Gilmore shouldn't have been a 1st ballot Hall Of Famer. Bob Lanier, Nate Thurmond, Willis Reed, and Bill Walton are all Hall Of Fame big men from around The A-Train's era. If you compare his numbers to those 4, there is no major statistical gap. In fact, his numbers trump all of theirs in points and rebounds in their pro careers. And if you go by what The A-Train did in his 2 years at Jacksonville, his case for induction becomes even more formidable.

It's more than The A-Train's combined ABA/NBA production of 24,941 points, 16,330 rebounds, and 3,178 blocks that commands respect. You have to look at his stature in the game. From the way he put his small school on the college basketball map by taking them to the 1970 NCAA championship game to leading the NBA in field goal percentage for 4 years straight and being the league's all-time leader in career field goal percentage. The A-Train's presence in the low post should not be discounted. Thankfully, a giant oversight was finally corrected in 2011.

Larry Kenon

-Missouri Valley Conference Player Of The Year (1973)
-ABA All-Rookie First Team (1974)
-3x ABA All-Star (1974-1976)
-ABA Champion (1974)

-2x NBA All-Star (1978-1979)

Larry Kenon is one of the least appreciated players in Spurs history, if not ever. In college he led Memphis to the NCAA title game in his only year there, losing to a Bill Walton-led UCLA team. In his rookie year in the ABA, Special K won a championship with the Nets alongside Dr. J. But Special K is best known for being one of the greatest players to make the transition from the ABA to the NBA. Many have suggested that without the trades that brought Special K, Billy Paultz, and Mike Gale to the Spurs in the summer of 1975, the Spurs might not have been able to make the jump to the NBA. With George

Gervin and James Silas already on the team, the addition of Larry Kenon gave the Spurs 3 All-Star quality players.

Larry Kenon is looked at as the Kawhi Leonard of his day, an elite 2-way player. In fact, he averaged 21.9 points and 11.3 rebounds per game for the 1976-77 season, making him the first player in Spurs history to average 20 points and 10 rebounds for a season. From 1974 to 1980, he was definitely one of the elite forwards in basketball. In that time frame he was 5th among all forwards in the ABA and NBA in points and steals, while coming in 3rd place for rebounds. Special K's averages in that time were 20 points, 10.5 rebounds, and 1.5 steals.

Special K had flair as a rebounder. He could snatch the ball out of the air with one hand and go the length of the court for an easy score. He was one of the first forward who could lead a fastbreak. He was the player that made those Spurs teams go. Special K was also a good defender, which he never got a lot of credit for. In a full display of his versatility, he had 29 points, 15 rebounds, and an NBA record 11 steals (tied by Kendall Gill in 1999) in a 110-105 Spurs win over the Kings on December 26, 1976.

Special K proved to be every bit of The Iceman's equal in the 5 years he played for the Spurs. With a nucleus of those 2 and Captain Late, the Spurs kept a high-powered offense and were always in the playoffs. The high point for those Spurs teams was reaching the Eastern Conference Finals in 1979. Special K had 4 straight seasons of averaging 20 points per game for the Spurs. The Iceman might have been lighting up scoreboards, but Special K was also having a lot of nights where he scored in the 30s and 40s. In his last regular season game with the Spurs, a 144-124 win over the Pistons on March 30, 1980, Special K had 51 points. That was his highest scoring game as a Spur.

In Larry Kenon's 5 seasons with the Spurs, he averaged 20.7 points, 10.3 rebounds, and 1.6 steals per game. Because of continuous contract troubles with the Spurs, he signed with the Bulls as a free agent in 1980. Before the 1980-81 season, Special K never averaged fewer than 34.6 minutes per game. His minutes went down to 28.1 in that first year in Chicago. His scoring also took a big hit, dropping to 14.1 points per game. That was Special K's last effective season. His scoring was basically cut in half the next season, down to 7.2 points. The 1982-83 season would be Special K's last, spending parts of the season with the Bulls, Warriors, and Cavaliers with a new low of 5.8 points per game.

Special K's career flamed out after he was released by the Cavaliers. The shockingly abrupt end to his career was unfortunate. Once again, at his best he was everything he bragged about himself being: a scorer, a good defender, a transcendent dunker, and an indispensable cog on those Nets and Spurs teams in the 1970s. With Larry Kenon being overshadowed by Julius Erving and George Gervin in his career, he never got the recognition he deserved and wound up being lost in the shuffle in the long history of pro basketball.

Mike Mitchell

-First Team All-SEC (1978)
-2x Second Team All-SEC (1976-1977)
-Third Team All-SEC (1975)

-NBA All-Star (1981)

Mike Mitchell was one of the NBA's greatest scorers of the 1980s. He finished the decade with the 10th most points scored in that period of time. If you only count 1980-1986, which were Mitchell's best years, it would put him at 7th. This list of prolific scorers includes Kareem Abdul-Jabbar, Moses Malone, Larry Bird, Alex English, and even George Gervin. His scoring during that time was methodical and effortless. During that stretch, he averaged 22.3 points per game while shooting 49.6% from the floor and 77.7% from the free throw line.

Mitchell's go-to move was a deadly mid-range jumper that he could release without consequence. At 6'7" and 215 pounds, he could get his shot up over other small forwards with ease and quick enough to take a bigger defender off the dribble. Mitchell played his college basketball at Auburn, becoming the school's all-time leading scorer and rebounder by the time he left. He was drafted 15th overall by the Cavaliers in the 1978 NBA Draft and showed some promise in his rookie year in limited action: 10.7 points per game on 51% shooting in just under 20 minutes a night.

Mitchell became the Cavs' starting small forward for the 1979-80 season as Stan Albeck took over as their head coach. Mitchell averaged 22.2 points, 7.2 rebounds, and just under a block and a steal per game. The next season he averaged a career-high 24.5 points and was rewarded with his only All-Star appearance. The 1980-81 season was Mitchell's last full season in Cleveland. Just after the start of the 1981-82 season Mitchell, who was the Cavs' only All-Star, was traded to the Spurs for Reggie Johnson and Ron Brewer. Cleveland would struggle for years to come while Mike Mitchell gave the Spurs new life.

In San Antonio Mitchell would rejoin coach Stan Albeck and have an immediate impact with the Spurs, teaming up with George Gervin and later Artis Gilmore to help the team win back-to-back Midwest Division titles. He and The Iceman made life easier for each other out on the wing, and Johnny Moore was a key contributor as well. In the 1984-85 season, Mitchell led the Spurs in scoring, which was the first time George Gervin hadn't done it since the 1975-76 ABA season. He averaged 22.2 points to Ice's 21.2 per game. From 1981 to 1988, Mitchell scored 9,799 points for the Spurs, which is the 7th highest point total in franchise history. He was in the NBA's top 10 in scoring 4 times and minutes played 3 times. Mitchell's career averages with the Spurs were 20.1 points, 5.5 rebounds, 0.7 steals, and 0.5 blocks per game.

Book Sources

*Loose Balls: The Short, Wild Life of the American Basketball Association - Terry Pluto, 1990 : Simon & Schuster

*Who's Better, Who's Best In Basketball - Elliott Kalb, 2003 : McGraw-Hill Books

*The Book of Basketball: The NBA According to The Sports Guy – Bill Simmons, 2009 : ESPN Books

*The Lawsuit That Saved The Spurs – Steve Peirce : San Antonio Lawyer Magazine (July-August 2015) : San Antonio Bar Assocciation

About The Author

Thomas E. Singleton Jr, iconically known as "Tom-Tom" (also has several other nicknames), steps into the arena of life to play his game at the highest level along with empowering others to achieve holistic success. He is a semi-pro football player, sports success journalist, radio personality, empowerment coach and author. He is passionate about seeing humanity at large reach their greater potential along with using sports as a vehicle to demonstrate effective leadership.

As an avid learner he has been afforded the opportunities to study at Alabama Agricultural & Mechanical University along with continued trainings and certifications in several areas such as finance, wealth creation, and human potential advancement through other esteemed platforms.

How To Contact The Author

For Speaking Engagements Or Special Appearances Contact:

www.facebook.com/TomTom82
tsingleton82@hotmail.com
tsingletonjr82@gmail.com
Twitter & Instagram: @TomTom0082

Made in the USA
Middletown, DE
26 May 2018